No Backbone!
The World of Invertebrates

Crafty Garden Spiders

by Nancy White

Consultant: Brian V. Brown
Curator, Entomology Section
Natural History Museum of Los Angeles County

BEARPORT
PUBLISHING

NEW YORK, NEW YORK

Credits

Cover and Title Page, © Robert Marien/Corbis/Superstock; 4–5, © Alain Christof/Oxford Scientific/Photolibrary; 6T, © Antonio López Román/age fotostock/SuperStock; 6B, © Hans Pfletschinger/Peter Arnold Inc.; 7, © Jeffrey Lepore/Photo Researchers, Inc.; 8, © Dwight Kuhn/Dwight Kuhn Photography; 9, © J.Kottmann/Peter Arnold Inc.; 10, © Peter Steiner/Alamy; 11, © David Cavagnaro/Visuals Unlimited; 12, © Dwight Kuhn/Dwight Kuhn Photography; 13, © Scott Camazine/Alamy; 14T, © B. Runk/S. Schoenberger/Grant Heilman Photography; 14B, © age fotostock/ SuperStock; 15, © Bill Beatty/Visuals Unlimited; 16, © Chelmodeev Alexander Vasilyevich/Shutterstock; 17, © age fotostock/SuperStock; 18, © Bill Beatty/Animals Animals-Earth Scenes; 19, © Roger Eritja/Alamy; 20, © Dwight Kuhn/ Dwight Kuhn Photography; 21, © Lawrence Stepanowicz/Alamy; 22TL, © Ray Coleman/Visuals Unlimited; 22TR, © Mike Kullen; 22BL, © Arlene Ripley; 22BR, © 2007 John Hartgerink; 22Spot, © Christian Musat/Shutterstock; 23TL, © Jim Wehtje/Photodisc Green/Getty Images; 23TR, © Bill Beatty/Animals Animals-Earth Scenes; 23BL, © Lawrence Stepanowicz/Alamy; 23BR, © Roger Eritja/Alamy; 24, © Christian Musat/Shutterstock.

Publisher: Kenn Goin
Editorial Director: Adam Siegel
Creative Director: Spencer Brinker
Design: Dawn Beard Creative
Photo Researcher: Beaura Kathy Ringrose

Library of Congress Cataloging-in-Publication Data

White, Nancy, 1942-
  Crafty garden spiders / by Nancy White.
     p. cm. — (No backbone! the world of invertebrates)
  Includes bibliographical references and index.
  ISBN-13: 978-1-59716-703-1 (library binding)
  ISBN-10: 1-59716-703-7 (library binding)
  1. Black and yellow garden spider—Juvenile literature. I. Title.

  QL458.42.A7W45 2009
  595.4'4—dc22
                           2008016622

For more information, write to Bearport Publishing Company, Inc., 101 Fifth Avenue, Suite 6R, New York, New York 10003. Printed in the United States of America.

10 9 8 7 6 5 4 3 2 1

Contents

Crafty Creatures

A garden **spider** spins beautiful webs.

The webs aren't just pretty, however.

They are deadly traps.

Insects that get caught in them soon become meals for the crafty spider.

Garden spiders make their webs in bushes, gardens, and grassy meadows.

Spinning Silk

A garden spider makes its web out of silk.

The silk comes out of tiny openings, called spinnerets, in the back of the spider's body.

The silk starts out as a liquid, but it dries as soon as it hits the air.

spinnerets

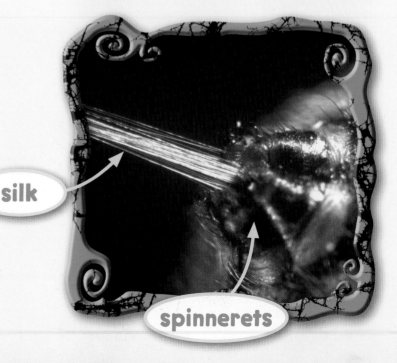

silk

spinnerets

Most spiders have two claws on each of their eight feet. A garden spider, however, has an extra claw on each foot that helps it pull the silk out of its body.

silk

Starting a Web

A garden spider begins its web with one thread of silk.

Sometimes the spider walks between two plants or twigs to attach each end.

Other times it lets the wind blow one end of the thread until it sticks to a twig or plant.

Then it attaches the other end to another spot.

The spider builds the rest of the web around this silk strand.

Spider silk is so thin that it is almost invisible. Yet it is as strong as a thread of steel that has the same thickness.

Finishing the Web

The garden spider works on its web for about an hour.

It keeps making silk and moving the whole time—at first in straight lines, and then in circles.

When the web is finished, the spider waits until it feels the silky strands shake.

Then it knows that an insect has gotten stuck in its sticky trap.

Garden spiders use sticky and nonsticky silk to make their webs. They don't get stuck in their webs because they walk only on the nonsticky parts.

Time to Eat

As soon as an insect gets trapped in the web, the garden spider rushes over.

Sometimes the spider wraps the insect in silk to keep it from moving.

The spider then bites and poisons the insect with its two fangs.

It also spits juices from its stomach onto its victim.

These juices turn the insect's insides into a mushy soup that the spider sucks up.

dragonfly

garden spider
wrapping a
fly in silk

Sometimes garden spiders
do not eat a trapped insect
right away. They wrap it in
silk and save it for later.

Helpful to Humans

A garden spider can poison and kill an insect with its fangs.

Yet its bite is not dangerous to people.

In fact, garden spiders help humans by killing insects that can be harmful.

For example, they eat grasshoppers that destroy crops.

They also eat mosquitoes that spread diseases.

grasshopper

mosquito

grasshopper trapped in web

Most female garden spiders are about one inch (2.5 cm) long and can eat insects twice their size. Male garden spiders are smaller than the females.

Hiding Out

Birds, frogs, lizards, and some kinds of insects, such as praying mantises, eat garden spiders.

A garden spider has crafty ways to hide from its enemies, however.

It can drop down from its web on a silk thread.

It may hang from the thread, out of sight, or hide under a leaf on the ground.

The spider can then get back up to its web by climbing up the thread.

praying mantis

garden spider

hairs

A garden spider knows when an enemy is coming near. The tiny hairs on the spider's eight legs can feel the slightest movement in the air.

Tiny Spiders

In the fall, a female garden spider makes a little bag, called an **egg sac**, out of silk.

She lays hundreds of eggs in it.

Tiny babies, called **spiderlings**, hatch out of the eggs in the spring.

They stay in the sac, however, until they grow bigger.

When the spiderlings are large enough, they tear a hole in the egg sac and crawl out.

egg sac

spiderlings

Like all spiders, garden spiders have a hard covering called an exoskeleton. In order to grow, a spiderling has to shed its exoskeleton and form a new, bigger one. This change—called molting—happens many times before a spider is full-grown.

Ballooning Babies

After leaving the egg sac, a spiderling climbs up to a high place, such as the top of a plant.

It makes a long silk thread, like a string on a balloon.

The wind catches the thread and carries the little spider up and away.

Wherever it lands, it will soon make a web and begin its life as a crafty garden spider.

silk thread

spiderlings ballooning

yellow garden
spider

There are about 76 kinds of
garden spiders. They live all over
the world. The most common kind
in the United States is the yellow
garden spider.

21

A World of Invertebrates

An animal that has a skeleton with a **backbone** inside its body is a *vertebrate* (VUR-tuh-brit). Mammals, birds, fish, reptiles, and amphibians are all vertebrates.

An animal that does not have a skeleton with a backbone inside its body is an *invertebrate* (in-VUR-tuh-brit). More than 95 percent of all kinds of animals on Earth are invertebrates.

Some invertebrates, such as insects and spiders, have hard skeletons—called exoskeletons—on the outside of their bodies. Other invertebrates, such as worms and jellyfish, have soft, squishy bodies with no exoskeletons to protect them.

Here are four spiders that are closely related to garden spiders. Like all spiders, they are invertebrates.

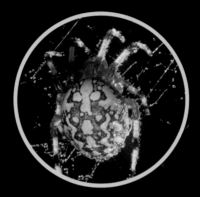

Marbled Orbweaver

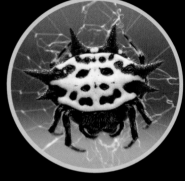

Spinybacked Orbweaver

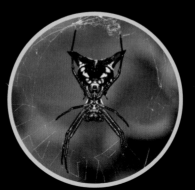

Arrowshaped Orbweaver

Basilica Orbweaver

Glossary

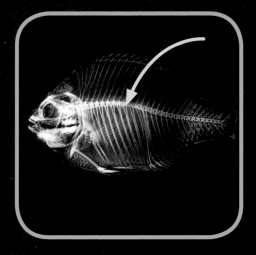

backbone
(BAK-*bohn*)
a group of
connected bones
that run along
the backs of some
animals, such as
dogs, cats, and fish;
also called a spine

egg sac
(EG SAK)
the silk container
that a female
garden spider
makes to protect
her eggs

spider
(SPYE-dur)
a small animal
that has eight legs,
two main body
parts, and a hard
covering called an
exoskeleton

spiderlings
(SPYE-dur-lingz)
baby spiders

Index

Read More

Cooper, Jason. *Garden Spiders*. Vero Beach, FL: Rourke Publishing (2006).

McGinty, Alice B. *The Orb Weaver*. New York: PowerKids Press (2002).

Learn More Online

To learn more about garden spiders, visit

www.bearportpublishing.com/NoBackbone-Spiders

About the Author

Nancy White has written many science and nature books for children. She lives in the Hudson River Valley, where she enjoys her garden and the creatures that share it—including the crafty garden spider.